Severe Weather: Storms

by Jacob Aarons

Scott Foresman
is an imprint of

Glenview, Illinois • Boston, Massachusetts • Chandler, Arizona
Upper Saddle River, New Jersey

ISBN 13: 978-0-328-51651-3
ISBN 10:   0-328-51651-1

4 5 6 7 8 9 10 V0FL 14 13 12 11

Thunderstorms, tornadoes, and hurricanes are kinds of severe weather. Severe weather can move trucks, smash houses, and wash away whole towns with gigantic waves. It can cause a great amount of **destruction.**

Learning about severe weather is the first step toward protecting ourselves from it. We can learn to prepare for severe weather by listening to and watching weather **forecasts.** An accurate forecast can give us the time we need to protect our families and homes from severe weather.

Thunderstorms

Thunderstorms often come from cold fronts. A cold front is caused by a cold air mass, or a cold body of air, meeting a slowly moving warm air mass.

Warm air is lighter than cold air. The heavier cold air sinks below the warm air. This forces the warm air to rise. The warm air becomes cooler as it rises. As the warm air cools, water vapor in the air condenses, or turns into liquid. Clouds form. The clouds become larger as more warm air rises.

The red arrows show warm air. The blue arrows show cold air.

Warm, moist air rises to form clouds.

As the clouds become larger, the drops of water in them become so heavy that they start to fall. At the same time, cold, dry air enters the clouds. This cold air sinks to the bottom of the clouds. It pulls the water down, and the water falls to the ground as rain. More cold air mixes with the warm air. The warm air cools and stops rising. Water droplets no longer form. The clouds become smaller and smaller, and the storm slowly ends.

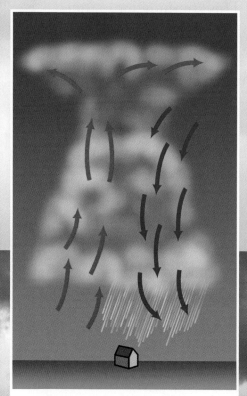

Water that forms in the clouds starts to fall. Colder, heavier air enters the clouds.

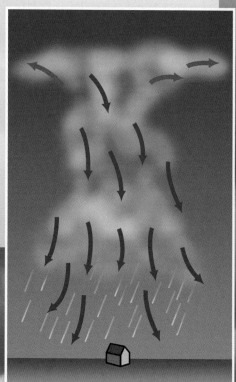

The cold air pulls the water down, making rain. The warm air can no longer rise.

Tornadoes

Tornadoes do not have as much energy as thunderstorms, but tornadoes can be more destructive than thunderstorms. Tornadoes can suddenly form within strong thunderstorms.

Before a thunderstorm fully develops, there can be a change in the speed and direction of the wind high up in the sky. This can cause a funnel cloud to form. A funnel cloud is a tower of spinning air that has the shape of a funnel. This spinning air gathers more and more power as the storm continues to draw moisture and warm air from below. The tornado forms when the funnel cloud touches the ground. Dust and debris give a tornado its dark color.

What makes a tornado so dangerous is that it is concentrated, or focused, energy. A tornado can have winds that blow up to three hundred miles per hour! Some tornadoes can travel up to one hundred miles! Many people who have lived through them say tornadoes approach very loudly and darken the sky. Tornadoes have been said to sound like trains or low-flying jumbo jets.

The winds inside
a tornado spin
very fast.

The winds of a tornado can rip the roofs off houses, destroy buildings, uproot trees, lift and toss automobiles, and **shatter** glass. Tornadoes can also blow tree branches, loose rocks, or broken glass so fast that they become deadly. The objects that are blown around by the fierce energy of a tornado often injure people and animals. Because tornadoes come from thunderstorms, they can also bring hail, heavy rain, and enough water to cause flooding– just as thunderstorms do.

Tornadoes can cause much destruction.

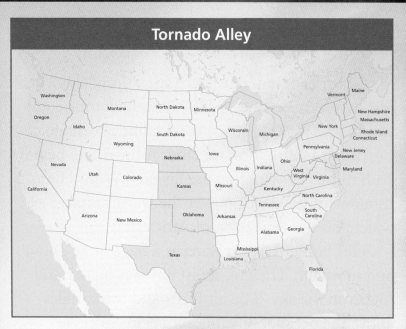

Tornado Alley

Nebraska, Kansas, Oklahoma, and Texas make up Tornado Alley.

There are some parts of the United States that are more likely to get tornadoes than other parts. One region that gets many tornadoes is called Tornado Alley. The states that make up this region are Nebraska, Kansas, Oklahoma, and Texas. If you live in one of these states, you can take steps to protect yourself from getting hurt by a tornado. An adult can help you find lists of helpful ideas using the Internet or your local library. During a tornado, it is important to go to a place that is underground or that has no windows.

Hurricanes

A hurricane can develop from a thunderstorm, just as a tornado does. Many thunderstorms come together to make a hurricane. Unlike a tornado, a hurricane cannot form on land. A hurricane begins with thunderstorms that are far out to sea. These thunderstorms develop over the warm tropical waters off the west coast of Africa.

This body of warm water is a big source of hot and moist air. The hot, moist air rises higher and higher in the sky. The air turns and twists miles above the ocean. Sometimes it begins to circle and move faster and faster in one direction. The thunderstorms join together to become a more powerful storm.

When the storm's winds blow at seventy-four miles per hour or faster, it is called a hurricane. The middle of a hurricane is called the eye. This middle area is peaceful, but all around it the storm continues to take warmth and moisture from the water below. When a hurricane begins to cross land or cool water, it loses power and fades away. But it does a great deal of damage as it begins to fade.

How a Hurricane Forms

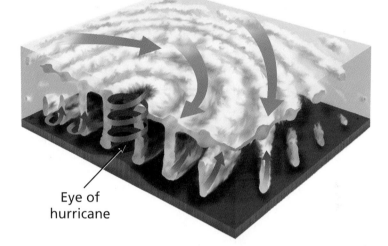

Eye of hurricane

When warm air rises (shown by the red arrows), a thunderstorm can form. Strong winds form in the storm. A hurricane forms when the winds (shown by the blue arrows) swirl at 74 miles per hour or faster. Storm winds spin around the eye of the hurricane (shown by the red spiral).

Eye of hurricane

The eye of a hurricane is the peaceful center of the swirling winds.

Hurricanes can be very destructive when they reach land. Perhaps you remember seeing pictures on the news of parts of the country where hurricanes have hit. The amount of rain that hurricanes can bring is enough of a reason to consider them a real problem for towns and cities along the coasts. They can bring anywhere from 5 inches to $2\frac{1}{2}$ feet of rain as they blow through! In areas where there are mountains and hills, people can be affected by the mudslides this amount of rain causes. A big mudslide can even push houses off cliffs. Hurricane winds can also cause destruction to homes, cars, buildings, and boats on the water.

Palm trees and water being blown in a hurricane

The most dangerous effect of many hurricanes is called a storm **surge.** A storm surge occurs when the winds of the hurricane cause the water level of the ocean to rise anywhere from eight to twenty feet higher than its normal level. The surge floods the land next to the ocean. Since many people like to build homes by the ocean, surges can cause much damage.

Surges do more than just cause the water level to rise and flood the land near the ocean. Surges also bring huge waves. These waves ride on top of the high water and cause even more damage **inland.** The waves that come with surges can be thirty-five feet high or more.

A hurricane hunter at work

Since hurricanes are able to do so much damage, many people believe it is important to learn as much as possible about them. Those who study hurricanes give us the forecasts we need to prepare for a storm and be as safe as possible. There are some scientists who fly a plane right into the eye of the storm to gather information. These men and women call themselves hurricane hunters.

These scientists hunt down hurricanes. Their work helps meteorologists, or weather forecasters, make better predictions. The information they gather helps hurricane researchers understand more about how and why hurricanes happen.

Flying right into the eye of a hurricane can be a bumpy ride! The eye of a storm is surrounded by an eyewall, which is a ring of thunderstorms. The clouds and the rain can be so thick that it can be hard for the crew to clearly see the wings of the plane! These scientists take risks to make discoveries about hurricanes for the safety of others.

Meteorologists make weather forecasts to advise us about when to expect severe weather.

Thunderstorms, tornadoes, and hurricanes are all powerful storms, and they all have the power to cause damage and possibly injury. This is why it is important to learn all that we can about these storms. With knowledge of what to do in severe weather, we can protect ourselves.

There are many resources that we can use to learn about severe weather. The Internet has many sites with helpful information. Some of these sites give us forecasts. Other sites let us know what to do when severe weather is coming our way. Libraries are great sources of information on safety. One of the most important steps we can take to protect ourselves is to make a plan of action.

A plan of action is a written set of directions to use in case of an emergency. The plan is clearly printed out and posted in a place where it is easy to see. This plan of action needs to be practiced. Act it out so that you will know what to do if there really is a tornado or hurricane headed your way.

Students in a
tornado drill

Just as we have fire drill plans, we should have
severe weather plans that fit the weather in our
area. For example, someone living in Tornado
Alley should probably have a tornado safety plan.
Making a plan to prepare for severe weather is not
too difficult. Your school may already have several
of them in place. You may have practiced what you
would do if a tornado or hurricane were **expected.**
Make sure you are familiar with the plan of action
used at your school and home. If you don't have a
plan of action at home, ask your parent or guardian
to help you put one together for the whole family.

We have learned about the causes and effects of three forms of severe weather. We have also learned that it is important to be prepared for severe weather by making a good plan of action. When we experience severe weather, we need to remember that it is part of nature. The planet Earth is amazing and powerful, and weather is an important part of it. Sometimes the weather is nice and we can imagine pictures in the shapes of clouds high over our heads. At other times these same beautiful clouds can become thunderstorms, and thunderstorms may then become other forms of severe weather. Respect for and knowledge of our planet's weather can help us to not only be prepared for the nasty effects of weather but to enjoy the beautiful days as well!

Glossary

destruction *n.* great damage; ruin.

expected *v.* thought something would probably happen.

forecasts *n.* statements of what is coming; predictions.

inland *n.* in or toward the interior.

shatter *v.* to break into pieces suddenly.

surge *n.* a swelling motion; sweep or rush, especially of waves.